Golden Numbers

A California Number Book

Written by David Domeniconi and Illustrated by Pam Carroll

Sleeping Bear Press™

310 North Main Street, Suite 300
Chelsea, MI 48118
www.sleepingbearpress.com

© 2008 Sleeping Bear Press is an imprint of Gale, a part of Cengage Learning.

Printed and bound in China.

First Edition

10 9 8 7 6 5 4 3 2 1

Library of Congress Cataloging-in-Publication Data

Domeniconi, David.
Golden numbers : a California number book / written by David
Domeniconi; illustrated by Pam Carroll.
p. cm.
Summary: "California's symbols, facts, landscapes, and history are
introduced using numbers. Each subject is introduced with a poem,
followed by more detailed information. Topics include volcanoes,
presidios, the desert tortoise, frogs, and monarch
butterflies"—Provided by publisher.
ISBN 978-1-58536-173-1
1. California—Juvenile literature. 2. Counting—Juvenile literature.
I. Carroll, Pam, ill. II. Title.
F861.3.D66 2008
979.4—dc22   2008009663

For Courtney Jade Davis

DAVID

❀

For Mary and John Ricksen,
who have inspired me by example to reach higher,
shine brighter, and believe in the goodness of humanity.

PAM

Here in California, we're friendly—most of us anyway. But California's State Marine Fish, the Garibaldi, is a bit of a grump.

This unfriendly fish lives in the warm shallow waters off Southern California, and if you happen to swim by, it just might come after you—even though it is only 14 inches (35 centimeters) long.

Making its nest among the rocks on the sea bottom, the Garibaldi lives alone and doesn't like visitors. To protect its nest, this fish will chase off larger fish and even divers by charging them and emitting a thumping sound.

Because of its bright orange color, the Garibaldi is popular with aquarium owners. Many of these orange fish were caught for fish tanks. California named the Garibaldi the State Marine Fish in 1995 and protected it from being fished in California waters.

one

1

1 Garibaldi,
a California fish who's known
to tell folks who drop by,
"I'd rather be alone."

Cable cars were invented to climb California hills.

San Francisco is a city of steep hills, hills too steep for a horse and wagon, which is how folks got around in the 1860s. In 1869, when Andrew Hallidie saw a horse and wagon slide down one of those steep hills, he came up with the idea of the cable car. Hallidie, an engineer, had built wire-cable bridges over the Sacramento River. He thought if trolley cars could be pulled by wire-cables running under the streets he could make travel safer on the city's steep hills.

The first test on a cable-driven car was in 1873. Not long after, cable cars like the ones in San Francisco were running in cities around the world. Today the cable cars in San Francisco are the only remaining manually operated cable cars. San Francisco's cable cars were almost retired in 1947, but the city voted to save the cable cars. In 1964 San Francisco's cable cars were designated a National Historical Landmark.

two

2

2 cable cars
climb up hills and never slip.
What can their secret be?
Don't panic; get a grip.

3 Pomo baskets,
always made by hand,
and each one guaranteed
to be a real Californian.

The Native Californians we call the Pomo are some of the world's finest basket makers.

Pomo baskets are prized by basket collectors and can be found in museums around the world. The Pomo have been weaving baskets for a thousand years, but few of their early baskets remain. In the early days baskets were destroyed when the weaver died. Only recently have baskets been saved. Today the tradition of basket making is kept alive by the relatives of the early weavers.

To show off their great skill, Pomo weave very small baskets. Some are only inches across, and some are so tiny they fit on the head of a pin. These extra-small baskets can only be seen with a magnifying glass. How the Pomo make baskets this small is a well-kept secret.

three
3

4 presidios
from San Diego to San Francisco Bay,
with a message for all pirate ships:
"Would you please just go away?"

San Francisco

Monterey

Santa Barbara

San Diego

Pacific Ocean

Sacramento River

San Joaquin River

Salton Sea

Along with the missions, the presidios were the first European outposts in California.

In 1769 when California was part of Spain, the Spanish began building adobe forts to protect the coastline. These forts were built at the best harbors, first in San Diego, and then in Monterey, San Francisco, and Santa Barbara. Life at the presidios was hard. Soldiers wore ragged uniforms and often went for a year without pay. Most presidio cannons were rusted and would not fire, and many of the soldiers had the wrong bullets for their rifles. In 1818 when the pirate Bouchard and his men attacked Monterey, the soldiers of the presidio were easily driven off and the pirates sacked the town.

Little remains of the presidios of Spanish California. But at El Presidio de Santa Barbara State Historic Park, you can see some of the original presidio, the second oldest building in California, which has been preserved and restored.

four

4

California has five active volcanoes.

Active volcanoes are volcanoes scientists believe could erupt, even though they have been quiet for thousands of years.

In the far northeast corner of the state, a range of low dome mountains make up the million-year-old volcanic area called **Medicine Lake**. One of California's tallest and most beautiful mountains, **Mount Shasta**, is actually a volcano. Another one of California's most beautiful mountains, **Mount Lassen**, is also a volcano. The **Clear Lake** volcanic field is the home of the world's largest geothermal field where steam captured from deep under the ground is used to create electricity. One of the world's greatest volcanic explosions happened 700,000 years ago in the **Long Valley** in the Sierra Nevada Mountains. For 40,000 years, the **Coso** volcanic field in Kern County has been quiet. But scientists believe one day it just might wake up.

5 volcanoes
whose names are good to know.
They may be sleeping peacefully now,
but then again they just might blow.

five

5

They say we're different in California. And that's the way we like it. Our sports are different, too. Lots of unusual sports had their beginnings in California.

When surfing began to be popular in the 1950s, some brave souls in Southern California put roller skates on wooden planks and rode them like surfboards on the hard streets, and skateboarding began.

In the 1970s, a group of daring young men put fat tires on old Schwinn bicycles, rode these bikes down the dirt trails of Mount Tamalpais in Marin County, and the sport of mountain biking was born.

Santa Monica was the place that first saw beach volleyball. The first games were played there in the 1920s and the first tournaments in the 1940s.

In San Diego in 1985, a surfer created a surfboard designed to be pulled by a water skiing boat, and wakeboarding was born.

six

6

6 skateboards,
this is how we play
when we want to have fun
the California way.

7 desert tortoises
are headed not so far away,
and should get where they're going
sometime next Tuesday.

Tortoises have been living in the California desert for millions of years.

That's not a home the desert tortoise carries around on its back. That shell is for protection. And they need protection—because with a top speed of 20 feet (6 meters) per minute, they aren't going to run away from anyone. Desert tortoises live in burrows, holes dug in the ground, where they lay their eggs and hide from the heat of the day. These vegetarians can live to be a hundred years old. And during all that long life tortoises will never venture more than a couple of miles from the burrow where they were born.

Roads and ranching in the desert have endangered the desert tortoise, the state reptile of California. In 1994 millions of acres of California desert were added to parklands to protect the tortoise. In the Mojave Desert, 39.5 square miles (102 square kilometers) have been set aside as the Desert Tortoise Natural Area.

seven

7

Can you guess which state, along with Alaska, has the most national parks? That's right, it's California.

In the Mojave Desert you will find a strange and beautiful yucca plant, the Joshua tree, at **Joshua Tree National Park**. Elephant seals and sea otters make their home in the **Channel Islands National Park**. In **Sequoia National Park** you can see General Sherman, the world's largest tree, with a trunk 103 feet (31 meters) around. **King's Canyon National Park** has the tallest mountain in the lower 48 states, Mt. Whitney, and a canyon deeper than the Grand Canyon. **Death Valley National Park** is the lowest place in the U.S.A., at 282 feet (86 meters) below sea level. One of the world's most beautiful valleys, **Yosemite National Park**, has four of the world's highest waterfalls. If you like boiling mud, steam, and sulfur, **Lassen Volcanic National Park** is just the place. Some of the world's tallest trees put down their roots at **Redwood National Park**.

eight

8

ELEPHANT SEALS AT CHANNEL ISLANDS

JOSHUA TREE

GENERAL GRANT AT SEQUOIA

KINGS CANYON

8 national parks,
places you must surely see.
The finest land in the Golden State,
and it all belongs to you and me.

HALF DOME, YOSEMITE

THERMAL STEAM AT LASSEN

COLLARED LIZARD AT DEATH VALLEY

REDWOODS

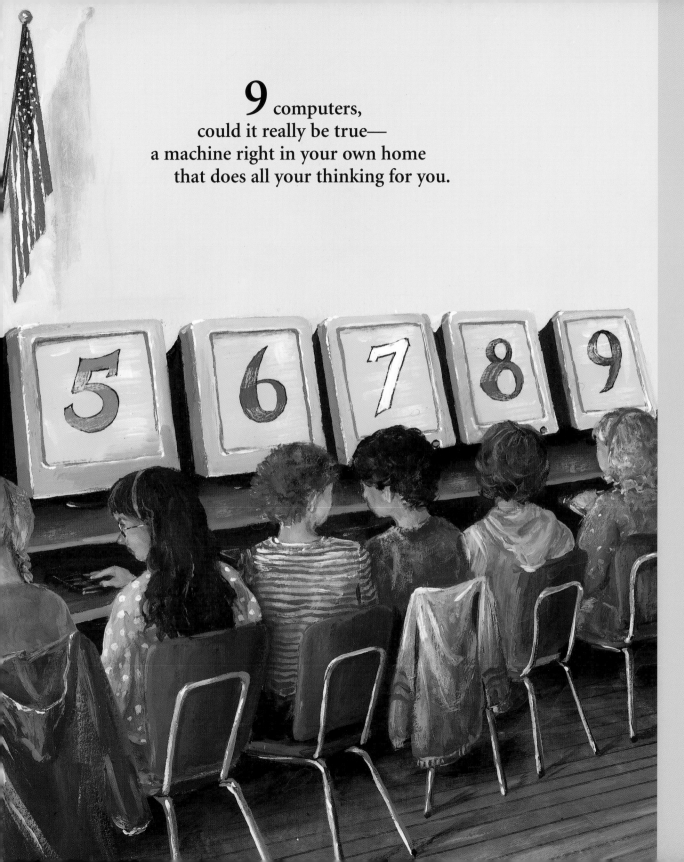

9 computers,
could it really be true—
a machine right in your own home
that does all your thinking for you.

The first home computers were built by two California nerds.

In 1977 in a garage in Mountain View, two twenty-year-old electronic whizzes built a computer, a computer unlike almost anything the world had ever seen. It wasn't a big expensive computer costing tens of thousands of dollars only big businesses could afford, and it wasn't a build-it-yourself computer for electronic types who read science magazines. It was a personal computer, the first computer created for families and small businesses. Steve Wozniak and Steve Jobs sold 500 of the Apple I. To get the funds to build their next computer, Wozniak and Jobs had to sell their prized possessions, a calculator and a Volkswagen van. The Apple II began the modern age of computers in homes, schools, and small businesses. It went on to become the most popular computer of the 1970s and 1980s, and the two electronic nerds became multimillionaires before they were thirty.

nine
9

Frogs come from near and far just to jump in California.

In 1865 Mark Twain wrote a story, "The Celebrated Jumping Frog of Calaveras County," about a gambler in the California gold country who would bet on anything, including jumping frogs.

Since 1932 a frog-jumping contest has been the main attraction at the Calaveras County Fair. Nowadays some 2000 folks and their frogs line up every year to see which frog can jump the farthest, and if anyone can break the world's record of 21 feet 5 inches (6.6 meters) set by Rosie the Ribeter in 1986.

ten

10

10 jumping frogs
always make a scene,
and do their very best
to keep California green.

In California we like railroad trains.

One of the biggest and best railroad museums in North America, the California State Railroad Museum, is in historic Old Sacramento. The museum's collection includes 19 steam-powered locomotives, 19 gas-powered locomotives, and dozens and dozens of passenger cars, freight cars, and cabooses. The museum's Southern Pacific No. 1 "C. P. Huntington," a steam locomotive built in 1863, helped in the construction of the transcontinental railroad, the first railroad across the United States.

On weekends at the museum you can take a ride on a steam-powered train along the Sacramento River.

11 locomotives,
and the world looks mighty fine
when a California engine
is moving on down the line.

eleven
11

12 fan palms
are just the spot
to stay cool as a cucumber,
because California is hot.

The California fan palm tree is the only palm tree native to North America.

Although the fan palm is found in the deserts of Southern California, these palm trees need water. So the trees grow near earthquake faults, places where water from springs deep underground comes to the surface. A palm oasis is a cool shelter from the desert heat. Under the shade of the palms, temperatures can be 10 to 20 degrees lower than they are out in the hot sun. These palm oases were the home of the native Californians called the Cahuilla. Besides using the fan palms for shelter, the Cahuilla ate the dark fruit of the palm tree and made clothing and shoes from the leaves.

twelve
12

20 state universities,
so let's all do our part.
Make sure you go to college,
and keep California smart.

Californians must be the smartest people in the world.

The California State University system, with 23 campuses from Humboldt to San Diego and 405,000 students, is the largest university system in the country. And the California Community College system, with 109 campuses and 2.5 million students, is the largest system of higher education in the world. And the University of California system with 10 campuses and 208,000 students, is one of the country's top institutions for higher learning and a model for higher education.

With so many colleges and universities, Californians can't help but be smart.

twenty
20

No matter what sort of landscape you like, you can probably find it in California.

California has snow. The deepest snow ever recorded, according to Guinness World Records, was 37.5 feet (11 meters) in 1911 in Tamarack. California has no snow. The desert in Death Valley is the driest place in the U.S.A. with less than 2 inches (5 centimeters) of rain a year. California has beaches. The Pacific coastline is 840 miles (1351 kilometers) long. California has mountains. Mt. Whitney, at 18,999 feet (5790 meters), is the tallest peak in the lower 48 states. California also has forests and rivers and valleys and islands and lakes—just about every sort of place you can imagine. You can play in the waves off Malibu beach one day and the next day be snowshoeing in the High Sierras.

No wonder everyone loves California.

thirty
30

30 feet of snow
and deserts and beaches and mountains of granite.
Is there any doubt about it?
California's the greatest place on the planet.

40 bedrooms—
how can it possibly be?
One house with so many;
it's a California mystery.

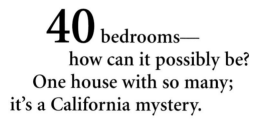

There are big houses, and then there are spooky big houses.

In 1884 Sarah Winchester began building her home in San Jose. She hired 22 carpenters to work twenty-four hours a day, seven days a week. And they didn't stop for 38 years. When Sarah died at the age of 83, she had created a house with 160 rooms, 1,257 windows, 467 doors, 47 fireplaces, and 40 bedrooms.

Legend has it Sarah Winchester built this house because she believed she was cursed. Her fortune had come from the Winchester rifle company, and many unfortunate souls had been on the wrong end of those rifles. Sarah believed she needed a house big enough to hold all those lost souls. So she added room after room after room. Legend also has it that these souls still live in Sarah's house. Today the Winchester Mystery House is a tourist attraction you can visit in downtown San Jose.

forty
40

The California condor is the largest bird in North America.

With a wingspan of 9 feet (3 meters), the condor can fly at 55 miles (88 kilometers) an hour and soar up to 15,000 feet (4572 meters) high. This big black bird has lived in California for thousands of years, from the time of the mastodon and saber-toothed cat all the way to the present day. But none of this could save the giant bird from our expanding human population. Buildings and power lines and pollution pushed the condor to the brink of extinction. In 1983 zoologists decided to capture the last few wild condors and breed them in captivity. For a time no California condors existed in the wild. The captured and bred birds were reintroduced beginning in 1992 and today there are 127 wild condors flying over California, Arizona, and Mexico. About 50 of these giant birds live in California.

Although condors are fierce-looking creatures, they never kill their prey. Condors only feed on dead animals.

fifty 50

50 California condors, perhaps you may have heard, flying over the Golden State are some mighty big birds.

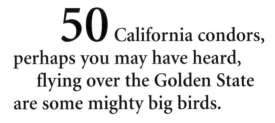

Was the road trip invented in California? No one knows for sure. But the motel was. And what's a road trip without a motel?

The Milestone Motel Inn, the world's very first motel, opened in San Luis Obispo in 1925. Before that time, folks had parked overnight in dusty auto camps. But now they had a new place to stay. It was called a "motel"—a combination of the words "motor" and "hotel." At the Milestone Motel you could drive right up to your front door. Today there are about 6000 motels in California, more than anywhere else. And why do we need so many motels? Because we have so many cars. There are more cars in California than in any other state. The good news is we can go anywhere we want. The bad news is air pollution. But the state of California has some of the toughest emission controls for automobiles in the United States. So we're working on it.

60 motels
with one just ahead you can bet.
So please don't ask the driver,
"Are we there yet?"

sixty
60

The world's first and most famous electric guitars come from California.

The Adolph Rickenbacker Company of Los Angeles was the first to build and sell an electric guitar, a 1932 Hawaiian guitar nicknamed the "frying pan." The Rickenbacker Company went on to make many kinds of electric guitars, and Rickenbacker's place in musical history was set in the 1960s when the Beatles hit the charts in the U.S.A. playing Rickenbacker guitars. Rickenbacker has been making electric guitars in Southern California for 75 years.

The world's most famous electric guitar, the Fender Stratocaster, was built by Leo Fender in Fullerton in 1954. The Stratocaster is the preferred guitar of many of rock and roll's greatest guitar players. Fender electric guitars are still made in Corona, California.

seventy
70

70 electric guitars,
so it shouldn't come as a shock.
In the Golden State
we know how to rock.

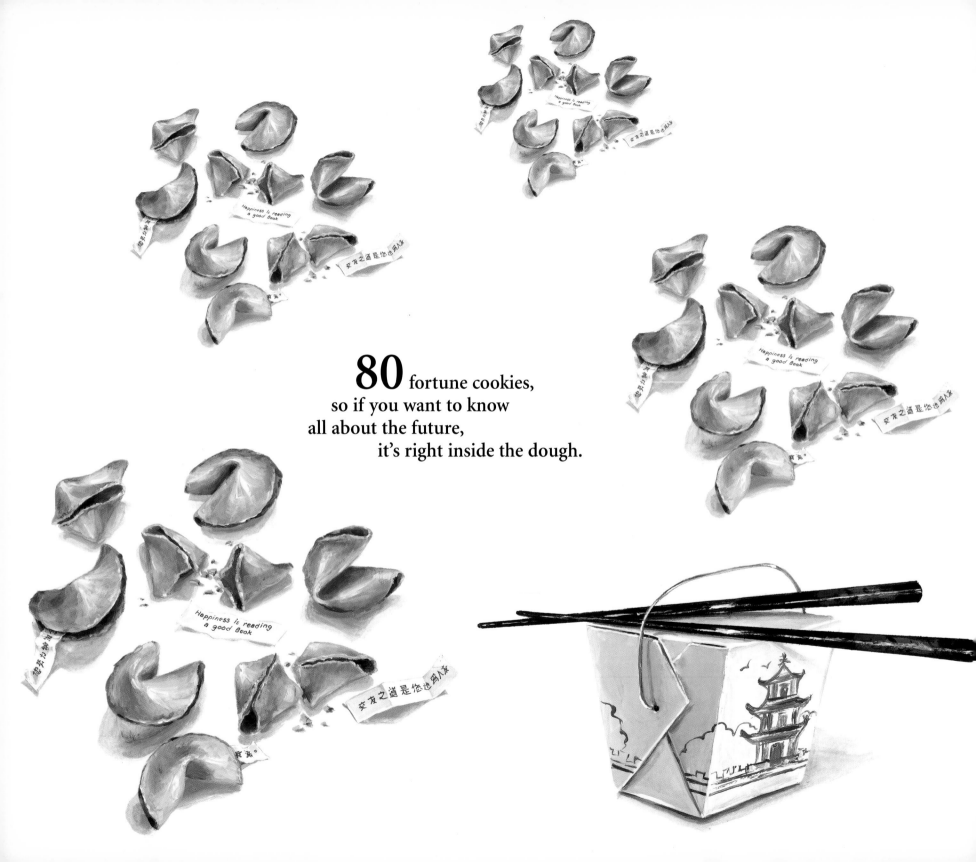

80 fortune cookies,
so if you want to know
all about the future,
it's right inside the dough.

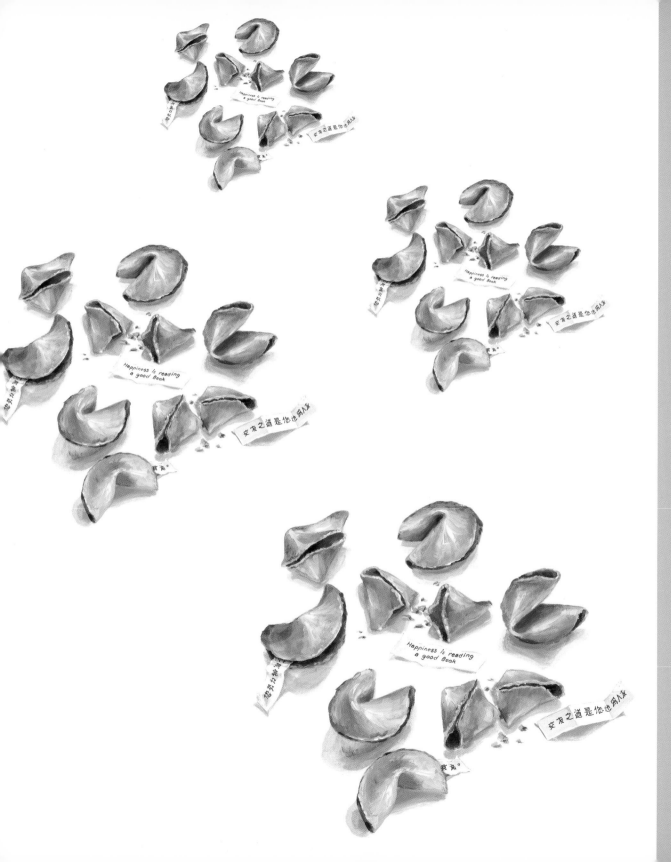

The fortune cookie was invented in Los Angeles. Or the fortune cookie was invented in San Francisco. You'll have to decide for yourself.

In 1918 in Los Angeles, David Jung of the Honk Noodle Company wanted to brighten the lives of poor people. So he made cookies with inspirational messages inside. He handed these cookies out to people on the street, and the fortune cookie was born.

Or, in 1914 in San Francisco, Makoto Hagiwara, the gardener who designed the Japanese Tea Garden in Golden Gate Park, wanted to thank the patrons who came to the park. So he put thank-you notes inside cookies, and the fortune cookie was born.

These are the two stories of the invention of the fortune cookie. So far no one has figured out which one is exactly true.

eighty
80

In California we like our vegetables.

That's because in California we grow more fruits and vegetables than any of the other 49 states. California's foggy Central Coast is the ideal climate for growing artichokes. Almost every artichoke grown in the U.S.A. comes from here.

California's Central Valley is one of the greatest food producing areas in the world. California grows most of the grapes, almonds, apricots, dates, figs, kiwi fruit, nectarines, olives, pistachios, and walnuts in the United States. And California is the number one state in growing avocados, melons, peaches, lemons, strawberries, and plums. Half the tomatoes in the world are grown in California. And let's not forget all our lettuce and lima beans.

So be a good Californian and eat your vegetables.

ninety
90

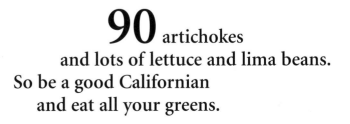

90 artichokes
and lots of lettuce and lima beans.
So be a good Californian
and eat all your greens.

If **100** monarch butterflies could write postcards,
they'd always add this line:
"Hanging out in the Golden State,
having a wonderful time."

Everyone likes to spend time hanging out in California—especially monarch butterflies.

Every fall millions of monarch butterflies from all over the western United States head west. Some traveling thousands of miles, they make their way for the eucalyptus, pine, and cypress trees of the California coast. There they gather by the thousands, hanging together in trees, fluttering like orange and black leaves. Pismo Beach has one of the largest winter colonies with over 100,000 monarchs. So many monarchs come to Pacific Grove the city's nickname is "Butterfly Town."

Year after year and generation after generation these butterflies return to the same trees. Scientists are not sure how the monarchs find their way to the same trees, but they think it might have something to do with scent. Or maybe like everyone else, monarchs just like California.

one
hundred
100

David Domeniconi

David Domeniconi grew up in San Francisco and graduated from San Francisco State College. He is the author of *G is for Golden: A California Alphabet*; *M is for Majestic: A National Parks Alphabet*; and *M is for Masterpiece: An Art Alphabet*. David and his wife, Janet, live the Alexander Valley near Healdsburg, California, where they own and operate an art gallery, J. Howell Fine Art.

Pam Carroll

Artist Pam Carroll embraces the traditional focus of realism and pictorial illusionism. *Golden Numbers* is her sixth children's book for Sleeping Bear Press. She lives with her husband, Chris, in Carmel, California where she paints daily and shows her work in several galleries throughout the United States.